The black book of Bitcoin

A Step-by-Step Bitcoin Guide on
Everything You Need to Know
About this New Currency

MARK JANNIRO

ISBN-13:
978-1519284525

ISBN-10:
1519284527
:

DEDICATION

This book is dedicated to my nephew Nicolas, a little boy who would see in his lifetime the future of altcurrencies to a degree we can only imagine..

CONTENTS

DISCLAIMER

.

INTRODUCTION

If you had invested $1,000 in Bitcoin 5 years ago in July of 2010, your money would have bought you roughly 16,660 bitcoins at $0.06. Today, July 2015, your bitcoins would worth close to $4,000,000. Not to mention that for a short period of time last year the price of Bitcoin surpassed $1,000. Imagine if you would have sold there.

I don't know of any other recent story in the financial markets with such a tremendous explosive power as Bitcoin. I can't think of any other investment that could have yielded such returns in such a small period of time.

Besides from the fact that Bitcoin has become so valuable, there's the fact that this alternative form of money has move from the underground worlds of programmers and hackers to the mainstream. However 99% of the population doesn't have any bitcoin, although many Surveys indicate that a majority of the people in the USA knows about Bitcoin, so there's still a huge potential and the life of Cryptocurrecies is just starting.

The question you might be asking, and believe me, we all do, might be:

Is it too late to invest in bitcoin? Am I late to the party? How can this Alternative Currency be a viable option to invest some money after such a crazy run over the last years?

Of course, no one has a magic ball and no one can tell you with a 100% security what is going to happen in the future. But in my eyes, the recent Bitcoin decline (from over $1,000 to around $240 that we have today) might prove to be the greatest opportunity to enter a more mature market that still has a tremendous upside for you as an investor and may prove to have many other advantages taking into consideration the future of the world economy, that right now stands in a very uncertain position.

If you want to better understand and become well versed in the Bitcoin subject, this book will guide you step by step so you can make an informed decision to become an investor or even a trader in Bitcoin.

The book has the basic knowledge to walk the walk and talk the talk in the Bitcoin subject, however it has also some deeper knowledge that you can simply skip if you aren't so interested in that particular area of the Bitcoin world. Many of the concepts are somewhat repeated or spoken over several times, since they are viewed in different angles. In general there are many aspects from the way Bitcoin works that are not so easy to grab at first, hence the need of treating them in different points of view.

So without any further delay let's jump in.

WHY BITCOIN?

E-commerce relies heavily on financial institutions that act as third parties in order to process payments done electronically. Although this system based on a trust-based model works for many transactions that are carried out over the Internet, it has some inherent flaws. For instance that, the transactions are not irreversible nor anonymous, as the financial institutions have to come between the parties involved in a transaction to mediate in case a dispute arises and this greatly increases the cost of the transaction and leaves room for fraud.

The need for a trust-based model arises due to the fact that in the current online model, transactions are reversible and you have to provide your personal data, so there is still a chance of fraud and costs are very high (think Paypal).

You can avoid this costs by carrying transactions using physical currency, however, in case of making an electronic payment; there is a need for a viable mode of exchange. There is the need of an electronic payment system, which instead of relying on a trusted third party operates using cryptographic proof. There is a need to reduce the instances of fraud, which can be achieved by making transactions irreversible and anonymous.

Another concern is the constant misuse of governments and central banks around the world of their local currencies. From hyperinflations to credit bubbles, to all kinds of manipulations, devaluations, capital controls and crazy taxations, we should really find a different way of storing our wealth, away from praying eyes and bureaucrats.

What we're talking about here is a new medium of exchange that can replace the traditional currency and make online transactions secure and private and that is Bitcoin; an innovative and novel solution that does not rely on financial institutions and yet is a secure way to carry out transactions.

Bitcoin can be defined as a crypto-currency, which means that the transfer and creation of bitcoin is dependent on an open source cryptographic protocol and does not rely on a central authority. This innovative currency option was introduced in the year 2008 as a peer-to-peer electronic cash system.

If you are wondering how the transfer of bitcoins takes place, it is a fairly simple procedure, and you can transfer them through any smartphone or a computer without a financial institution acting as an intermediary.

Bitcoin is becoming a rage around the world; originally, people supported the concept of bitcoin because they wanted to be a part of a revolutionary idea, however, people soon realized the potential of bitcoin and how it could grow into something huge. As more people began to take an interest in bitcoin, the prices started to inflate and the media attention that it got from its skyrocketing prices resulted in more attention being diverted to bitcoin from around the globe, and it became a mainstream sensation.

Many people believe that bitcoins have the potential to become an alternative medium of exchange if more and more people start trusting the bitcoin system rather than the central authority, for instance, the government. If you are wondering about how bitcoins can replace traditional currency and how they are different from regular currency, then you should definitely keep reading.

Why is bitcoin gaining popularity worldwide? It is simply because of the fact that it offers concrete benefits to users. Bitcoin enthusiasts rightly point out that, if stored properly, Bitcoin is potentially the most secure and the safest way to store private money, because it is digital and unlike physical currency there are no issues related to storing and the risk of theft can easily be minimized.

What truly sets bitcoin apart from traditional modes of transactions is that it addresses the drawbacks presented by the traditional currency. For instance, if we talk about cash, it does offer us the benefit of making or receiving payments without disclosing our identity and it is also portable, however the downside to using cash is that in order to make a transaction with cash, you have to carry it from one place to another and also you are relying on fiat money. In addition to this, another traditional mode of transaction is through credit cards, which employ trust based models. Although they enable you to send and receive money from all over the world, however, the issue with these electronic payment medium is that you have to provide your real identity if you want to carry out a transaction and normally you will have to pay fees for using this systems.

Bitcoin, on the other hand is free from all these drawbacks, and it is a secure way to make a transaction instantaneously in any part of the world without revealing your real identity and paying a minimum fee and, if moving money abroad, saving a lot in exchange rate fees.

Popular opinion over the future of bitcoin varies considerably, since there are many who are suspicious about how bitcoin works and are hesitant to invest in it. At the same time, there are others who strongly believe that it is the currency of the future and a mode of payment best suited for this age of technology.

Currently, it does seem that the increasing popularity of bitcoin is due to the perception that it is an anonymous way to carry out transactions without coming under the watch of the government, the banks or any third party institution.

Our world today needs a currency that can be truly global in nature and bitcoin is an ideal form of currency in that sense. It functions like cash or traditional currency, however, its use is not tied to the identity of the person who is making the transaction and any transactions that you make with bitcoin become untraceable and irreversible.

The success of bitcoin is evident from the fact that Overstock.com started accepting bitcoins as payments and following their lead many major companies started doing the same including Microsoft, Time Inc., and Dell. Bitcoin is rightly said to be the currency of the future.

WHAT IS BITCOIN?

Bitcoin can be simply defined as a novel payment system, which relies on digital money. It is a decentralized peer-to-peer electronic cash network that operates without any intermediary authority. In easier terms, bitcoin basically functions as cash for the Internet transactions. It allows you to send money from any part of the world and all you need is a working Internet connection to do so, the transaction costs are negligible and its added benefits include anonymity, irreversibility of transaction and complete decentralization.

Bitcoin is basically a new type of currency, which was created in the year 2008 by an anonymous person who used the pseudonym Satoshi Nakamoto. It completely revolutionized the way transactions are done; with using bitcoin, there is no need of a middleman so you get rid of banks; there are no transaction processing fees and you do not have to give your name in carrying out a transaction, so you gain complete privacy. As bitcoin enables you to carry out peer-to-peer transactions, a payment made through bitcoin will reach its recipient in no time. You can send money in the form of bitcoins to any part of the world without paying any processing fees, and you can also have an option to pay a small processing fee, which will allow you to process your transaction faster. You can manage bitcoins by using pseudonyms, and the receiver only needs to provide his/her bitcoin address and the sender can send the bitcoins.

Many people are of the opinion that bitcoin is the most volatile form of currency around the globe, yet 100,000 bitcoin transactions are taking place each day and this number continues to grow.

Bitcoin is a relatively new idea. In August 2008, Neal Kin, Charles Bry and Vladimir Oksman filed an application for a patent of Bitcoin and they denied having any links to Satoshi Nakamoto, who is supposed to be the creator of Bitcoin. In the same month, these three individuals also registered a site named Bitcoin.org.

In the coming months, Satoshi Nakamoto released a white paper written by him, which revealed his idea of a peer-to-peer system of electronic cash transactions. According to him, his idea will enable people to send and receive money without the need for a trust based third party, and this paper provided the foundation for bitcoin.

In the year 2009, the first block by the name of Genesis was launched, which began the process of mining bitcoins. The first ever transaction using bitcoins took place in January 2009, between Satsoshi Nakamoto the developer, and Hal Finnety who is a cryptographic activist. Later in the same year Hong Kong opened to the general public, the first bitcoin counters.

In August 2010, bitcoin faced its first setback, as it was hacked and generated 184 billion additional bitcoins, which resulted in lowering currency value. In October another controversy surrounded bitcoin as a report published by an inter government group pointed out that this new mode of transaction could make money laundering easier and the report stated that through this new currency individuals can even sponsor and finance antigovernment or even terrorist organizations.

In March 2013, efforts were made to regulate bitcoin and in order to do so; the U.S. Financial Crimes Enforcement Network issued a report to regulate bitcoin. The report was aimed at helping people who were engaging in the exchange of virtual currency.

The year 2013, proved to be a turning point for bitcoin as the market touched the 1 billion dollar mark and Bloomberg openly endorsed it by stating that bitcoin can be used in place of real currency to carry out transactions like the buying of goods and services.

In the same year, the People's Bank of China banned the use of bitcoin for transaction purposes and stated that it is not real currency and hence does not have a similar legal status. This ban was indicative of the threat that bitcoin presented to China's control over capital and its financial strength.

In the year 2014, bitcoin touched another milestone, as HMRC classified it as private money, which meant that no value added tax will be charged on the exchange and mining of bitcoins. In the same year Microsoft, the tech giant with which all of us are familiar, started to accept bitcoins as a mode of payment.

It is obvious that the future of bitcoin is bright and with the help of tighter regulations, we can assume that there will be extensive adoption of bitcoin as an alternative currency by bigger institutions.

Bitcoin is simply an alternative form of currency, so what benefits does it offer to a regular individual like you and me? First of all, it provides freedom. It enables you to send and receive money in the form of bitcoins from any part of the world, and you do not have to worry about any bank holidays, capital controls, borders between countries or limits imposed by any third party. Bitcoin enables you to have full control of your money.

Payments made via bitcoin do not require any processing fee, though you may wish to pay a small fee, which will ensure that your transaction is processed and confirmed faster. As stated earlier, transactions made using bitcoin are secure and safe, they are irreversible and do not have any sensitive data like your personal details. As a merchant it also gives you a chance to expand into unexplored markets where there is no facility of credit cards or chances of fraud are high. As a merchant with bitcoin, you enjoy lower processing fees, less administrative expenses and access to larger markets.

Using bitcoin as a mode of transaction enables you to have complete control over your transactions, it is not possible to add charges in later stages of transactions, and payments can be made without sharing any personal information, thus, safeguarding against identity theft.

Transparency is a guaranteed feature of bitcoin, and information related to the money supply is available on the block chain. You can look at it and verify it instantaneously. As the protocol is cryptographically protected, no institution or individual can manipulate or influence it. Thus, you can trust bitcoin as being fully transparent, neutral and predictable.

THE PRESENT ECONOMY

These days, the need for virtual currency is undeniable. Every transaction, which takes place online, needs either virtual currency or credit to process.

While transactions via normal mediums require exchange fees, have possible payment delays and charge taxes, Bitcoin gives you the same guaranteed security with none of the time wasted in processing and extra fees.

Bitcoin is easy to use and once you get the hang of it, there is nothing like it! Unlike other payment methods like credit cards, which require you to give your credit card number and security information, Bitcoin requires nothing of the sort and authorizes a transfer of a specific amount only.

Since Bitcoin is independent and not a government controlled currency, it is considered an alternative to the Dollar or the Sterling Pound. However, in reality over the course of the last four years, Bitcoin's value has fluctuated quite a bit.

Bitcoin finishes off the worry of credit card fraud as no information about your credit card and security needs to be given. Moreover, there are countries where credit card payments are not even accepted. These countries can use Bitcoin and be connected to the world economy and stop losing out. Recently in countries like Argentina or Venezuela, where the local governments enforce capital controls and exchange rate regulations, Bitcoin has proven to be a good alternative for the people to move their money around and bypass their nonsensical government policies.

It is possible that either Bitcoin or other alternative currency will eventually replace a good part of other payment methods since people have found it to be a reliable and independent way of storing wealth.

Credit card companies manage billions of dollars in transactions. If Bitcoin companies manage to provide a solution simple enough for many people to use, the demand of Bitcoins could increase dramatically when it starts to claim a bigger piece of the multi-billion dollar market

CAN BITCOIN REALLY REPLACE MONEY?

It might happen sometime in the future to some degree but it is highly unlikely that it will happen soon to a larger scale. If governments truly saw a real threat from Bitcon in the immense power of manipulation they have today controlling the economy by manipulating the national currency, most likely they would try to stop Bitcoin, like it already happened in China. However if people really start using it on a grand scale, governments simply will not have the power to stop it and will try to find ways around it, like taxing it.

It is possible that even if people are not ready to leave traditional transaction methods, they are still willing to use Bitcoin as an alternative to other options available online or simply as a method to store wealth in a secure anonymous environment. This means that they might not let go of their currency notes and credit and debit cards but they may agree to use Bitcoin as an alternative to other online payment methods like PayPal. However, this too will only be possible if Bitcoin shows that it is effective and stable at least like the other options available. But that will only happen over time.

Even if Bitcoin does not completely replace currencies, it may yet become successful. When it becomes a popular option with customers to pay for their transactions, this will put pressure on banks and credit companies to bring down their costs in order to be more competitive with Bitcoin. And if they fail to do so, they may become almost obsolete online and everyone will just start using Bitcoin.

One of the biggest flaws of Bitcoin pointed out by many is that its deflationary character may lead people to start hoarding it, thus creating an artificial shortage of it for trading or investment. This is uncommon in any form of fiat currency however, one must remember that before the 20th Century many currencies, even the US dollar used to be deflationary, so people had good reasons to save it. Because of these reasons many people compare it to gold.

Some people believe that the problem could be that the customers will put off a lot of purchases to the future. These customers reason that the price of the item will be cheaper in the future and thus it will be a smarter decision to buy it then. However a counterargument put forward against this point is that people need some things immediately. We buy new computers frequently because of the evolving technology , since we need access to that technology now, even though we could have bought an even advanced computer in the future for the same price. The desire of needing an object now cannot be ignored. The real target of this deflationary force is in the way of an economy, focused on the demands of customers, rather than on only maximizing purchases. As usual, the market makes required adjustments with any problem, if left in peace to do its job.

The need for a market that is as efficient as it can be is not only restricted for a Bitcoin economy but for any kind of economy. While there is freedom of information, there also needs to be an absence of non-market influences on the economy as well. One of these influencing factors includes the question of survival, as free markets operate best in prosperous societies.

.

INVEST YOURSELF IN BITCOIN

The simplest and most obvious way to begin investing in Bitcoin is to buy some. It is now very easy to buy Bitcoins (BTC) as they are established firms that deal in BTC buying and selling worldwide. For US citizens, a convenient solution would be Coinbase. It is a company that sells Bitcoins at a mark-up value of approximately 1 percent above the present market price.

Americans and some other countries have the added facility to link up their bank accounts with their Coinbase wallet so they can easily transfer between their bank accounts and their Coinbase account where they can buy and sell bitcoins. Customers also get offers to buy BTC after regular intervals. For example, people who want to buy BTC as soon as they receive their monthly salary can use the auto-buy option, which will do it for them. A few precautions should be taken before using the service though. After an auto-buy order is issued, the price of the BTC when it is bought is not in the user's control. Also, another cause for concern is that the company does not offer exchange, rather only buying or selling BTC from Coinbase because the firm sources Bitcoins from other customers. This may result in delays or technical issues in extremely liquidity-sensitive market moves.

If you are looking to trade and want to exchange Bitcoins instead, choose BitStamp for your BTC needs. Users trade amongst each other and not with the company because it is only the middleman in this transaction. Bitcoins are extremely liquid goods and there is almost always a person who will accept your offer to trade. The fees for this service starts at 0.5 percent it will be reduced to 0.2 percent if you happen to trade more than $150,000 in 30 days.

If that does not appeal to you either then there are other ways too. Bitcoins can be bought offline as well through a website called Local Bitcoins. The website helps sellers find potential buyers or vice versa. The bitcoins have already been collected from the seller and locked into escrow. They can only be released to buyers. Again, the usual precautionary measures when meeting strangers should be taken and in case an issue arises, one should file a dispute with the company after 24 hours.

REASONS TO INVEST

Investing in Bitcoins is a very unconventional way to use your money and it may leave you confused about whether it is the right choice. Although individual advice is not given and you should perform your own research and make your investing decisions based on your personal situation. The answer is normally positive since investing it in the unusual Bitcoin could be a way of gain maximum returns in the long term, and above all it could prove to be a way to safeguard part of your savings from yet unknown uncertainties from future times.

There were a number of stories circling in the mainstream media for the past few months, hinting that Bitcoin is a potential bubble. It was during that period that Michael A. Robinson was amongst the few technical analysts that stood steadfast to their belief that the Bitcoin market was healthy and had a bright future ahead.

Another reason to invest is that it is safe from counterfeit and fraud. Now you may be thinking that since Bitcoin is a digital currency and digital data is so easy to copy, how can that be possible? The answer is the brilliant creator Satoshi who made the list of all transactions public via a public file listing all the transactions called the Block Chain. This way, before confirming a transaction, the Bitcoin's validity is verified by confirming that the currency has not been previously used. This ensures that there is no double spending, which is a simple yet effective method.

You shouldn't worry about being sold a counterfeit or fake BTC because it is not possible that your wallet would accept it, or even that it can be sent in any way to you.

The BTC economy is quickly making its mark in the world. The BTC that was worth decimals of a penny in its humble beginnings is now fluctuating around $250 and reached over $900 about a year ago.

Security analysts, experts and others who advocate for digital freedom have nothing but praise for BTC, as its system is one of a kind and has opened the door to new opportunities. Also the list of transactions is anonymous and this helps people feel secure about their private spending.

The value of BTC is subject to frequent and wild fluctuations and all this can happen in a day. Matt Elbeck, Troy University's marketing professor co-authored a study with Chung Baek, his colleague. During July 2010 and February 2014, the price of the Bitcoin was more volatile than many of the competing digital currencies.

The mishaps and unfortunate incidents such as BTC with half a billion dollars disappearing from Mt. Gox (Discussed in detail in the next section), have been adding uncertainty in the minds of investors. However I wouldn't worry about a company dealing with bitcoins crashes since that could, and has happened many times, with companies that manage regular currency. I'd rather worry to research good companies for my Bitcoin needs.

There has been much speculation and rumours about the Bitcoin viability, and although it's not a perfect currency (none of them are), it has been perfected and many of the holes it had in the past have been closed.

BTC has proven to be very successful for some investors, especially for those who have entered early in to this trend. There are dozens of stories of people who bought a few hundred bitcoins (or even a few thousands) when they could be traded for around $0.20, only a few years ago, suddenly finding that their old hard drives in the basement had real fortunes worth of bitcoins.

There is still growth potential in the Bitcoin realm. A lot of interest has being generated amongst investment firms who are excited about the new currency and the technology that makes it work. This will lead to an even wider demand for digital currencies that will increase as the currency becomes mainstream.

In conclusion, if you are not afraid of taking some risks and believe like me, that the central banks controlled currencies we have today might have a major collapse in a close future, it could be wise to diversify your savings and add some Bitcoin to the mix. I wouldn't be crazy about it and bet the farm, but if you accumulate steadily a comfortable amount for you, maybe in a few years you could be glad you did.

THE SETBACKS

Bitcoin has faced quite a few setbacks since its inception. It does not have a good reputation amongst journalists and economists but that is mostly because of their clients and how they are abusing the power of the digital currency. NYT columnist, Andrew Ross Sorkin, went as far ahead as calling Bitcoin an inferior form of gold at best that only an alien would even consider buying. Not only this, he is against digital currency all together and believes it would lead to chaos and anarchy.

Another setback bitcoin has to face occasionally is the distributor of Bitcoin turns out to be a fraud. One such example is Charlie Shrem, co-founder of BitInstant, who was convicted of money laundering linked to the virtual black market, Silk Road. It is reported that he played his part in helping drug sales, completely aware of the implications but ignoring them in the quest for substantial profits. The exchange service, BitInstant was permanently closed and Shrem, the vice-chairman handed in his resignation to the Bitcoin Foundation.

This is not where Bitcoin's dark period ends; it had to face three more losses: Apple brought out the big guns and removed the one and only Bitcoin wallet app left from the App Store without a valid reason. After two days, various sources revealed that Russia had banned bitcoin on the basis of an increasing interest in the cryptocurrency and its role in money laundering via illegal means.

The biggest setback however, remains to be the incident at MtGox, Tokyo which can never be lived down. Hacking into one of bitcoin's oldest exchange center affected the bitcoin's entire ecosystem. The hacker still remains unknown but used a glitch in the protocol to complete the task. The spill over effects caused bitcoins withdrawals to be suspended for the entire day. The glitch was not identified and bitcoins worth 0.5 billion US dollars disappeared from the exchange.

Most analysts agreed that a technical malfunction of the original code is what went wrong with the system, which is not as major as the previous issues digital currencies had to face. However, they also said that these glitches should not return because their reoccurrence will have a negative effect on the confidence of users and they will not see bitcoin as a reliable and stable currency.

In simple terms, it is similar to hackers breaking into the Federal Reserve and draining the confidence of users in the official monetary system. The number of affected people is lesser in the case of Bitcoin though.

On the other hand, MtGox announced that there were no unusual and exploitable features in the key protocol that their software could report but has yet not resumed withdrawals. This has briefly summarized the incident. The bitcoin community was enraged with MtGox because they usually did not respond to customers and had shady relationships with their banking client.

Prior to the hacker's attack, a warning was received. Wall Street was not pleased with Bitcoin because of its rouge and untraceable character. Investors were advised to limit their exposure to Bitcoin and not use it for exchanges or as a store of value.

However JP Morgan argues that no government is likely to accord bitcoin a legal tender status. He also said that Bitcoin and other cryptocurrencies should not reach the level for it to be worth promoting their use for payments, investment or commerce.

The biggest trading platform for Bitcoin in India has shut down their company after the citizens were made aware by the central bank of the risky nature of virtual money. BuySellBitCo.in has suspended operations and it was confirmed after their currency's value went down by more than 50 percent.

China's central bank issued a similar warning to the Chinese and the biggest trading platform there banned deposits in Yuan. The People's Bank of China ordered all financial institutions to refuse provision of Bitcoin and its relevant services and informed the citizens about its money laundering uses. The dollar value of one bitcoin has shot as high $1,200 but returned to its previous level after the Chinese central bank issued their warning. Standing now in June 2015 around $250.

BuySellBitCo.in officially reported that they had suspended buying and selling Bitcoins until they can come up with a clearer framework to work with. They also said that the action was taken to protect the customers and their interests.

Bitcoin can be stored virtually on any mass storage device and offers anonymity when it comes to making payments. It started getting popular in India and has now established itself as a preferred method of exchange although their tradition states all assets should be backed by tangible goods like gold, making bitcoin a good second best.

Virtual currency not being backed by any asset or government and having a value subject to constant speculation caused the central bank of India to speak out. At some point India was close to ban bitcoin and it's alternatives.

THE TERMINOLOGY AND BASICS

Let's dissect the steps; terminology and processes involved in the Bitcoin System to help you better understand how this whole thing works. The following chapter is a sort of glossary that will help you get a better grasp and become more literate on the subject. However many of the most important subjects will be treated in more depth in further chapters from this book.

BITCOIN

Is a payment system operating on an online Open Source environment which allows monetary transactions in between users (peer-to-peer) and it's not controlled, owned or ruled by any central bank, company, government, single administrator or authority. It is operated and maintained by other users who provide their own computational power to make transactions happen. These users are called miners, because they get a reward in bitcoin by providing this computational power, miners are also responsible for adding the layers of encryption that allow the bitcoin processes to be secure and impossible to hack or counterfeit.

BLOCK CHAIN

Block chain refers to the public record or database containing all the Bitcoin transactions. The transactions are organized in a chronological order. All the Bitcoin users have access to the block chain. It helps in verifying the stability of the Bitcoin transactions; so double spending can be prevented.

BLOCK

Block refers to a record in the Block chain, which confirms and contains numerous waiting transactions. On average, one new block along with transactions is added to the Block chain six times per hour via the process of mining.

BTC

It is a commonly used unit that designated one Bitcoin. It is represented by B.

DOUBLE SPEND

Double spending refers to the phenomenon when a corrupt or malicious user tries spending their Bitcoins with two dissimilar recipients at one same time.

CONFIRMATION

When a certain transaction is processed by Bitcoin's network and cannot be reversed, this phenomenon is known as 'confirmation.' Confirmation is received by a transaction when it is made a part of a block.

CRYPTOGRAPHY

It is an important division of mathematics. It helps us in creating mathematical proofs for enhancing the network's security. Online banking and commerce commonly rely on cryptography for making their networks and portals fool-proof. In Bitcoin, cryptography helps in preventing anybody to distort a block chain and spend funds using somebody else's wallet. It is also used for encrypting wallets so they are impossible to access without the proper password.

PUBLIC KEY CRYPTOGRAPHY

When you make use of the exact same password for encrypting and decrypting something, this phenomenon is known as 'Symmetric-Key Encryption.' Two dissimilar passwords are made using 'Public key cryptography.' Anything, which is encrypted using one password, can be easily decrypted with the other one. One is chosen to work as the 'private key' so you need to keep it a secret. The other password is used as 'public key' so you can broadcast it to others.

HASH RATE

Hash rate is the term used to calculate the processing or calculating power of the hardware used to keep the Bitcoin network going. Miners use their hardware, which has x Hash Rate power to solve and process the needs of the Bitcoin newtork. The network needs to make huge and complex mathematical operations for staying secure and that processing power is measured in hash rates. For example, when this network makes around 10 trillion different calculations in a second, it hash rate reads 10 Th/s.

WALLETS

Wallet is a term used to represent a person's account on the Bitcoin network. It's a piece of software containing your credentials to access your Bitcoin funds. Your wallet is comprised of your public and private keys. A Bitcoin wallet shows you the balance of the Bitcoins it keeps and also enables you to pay or receive Bitcoin by generating a unique Adress that will be used to complete the transaction.

ADDRESSES

The public keys are also known Bitcoin addresses. When you send a BTC to anyone at their Bitcoin address then all those on that network can see what you did. However, only the owner and holder of that address and its private key are able to spend that BTC. A bitcoin address can be represented by a long string of characters or by a QR Code. See it as your account number in your bank. You could publish your account number, but only you will have access to the funds.

TRANSACTION

BTC can only exist in a transaction and not on any address. When you spend a BTC, you drain one or many input transactions. You are also sending that particular BTC to many or one output address. A transaction is finalized when it is made part of a block. When you include the transaction fee, you ascertain that you will be included in a miner's block.

MINING

Mining is basically the process of record keeping that keeps Bitcoin reliable, it's achieved by using computer hardware to carry out mathematical processes and calculations for the Bitcoin's network for confirming transactions and providing the security of the network via encryption. Bitcoin miners collect a transaction fee for all the transactions confirmed by them. Mining is specialized as well as competitive. Not every Bitcoin user practices mining. Also, mining isn't an easy or simple procedure of making money since it requires expensive and top of the line hardware and a good knowledge of the Bitcoin system.

DIFFICULTY

Miners have a monetary reward when they solve a block, so the Bitcoin system was designed to add a level of difficulty after 14 days, hence increasing the difficulty for the miners to get their job done according to the overall performance of the network. Making the reward more and more desirable and hard to get as the mining power becomes greater and more competitive.

POOLS

Block solving is a laborious and complex process, but it can be made a little more convenient and attainable by becoming a part of a pool. Upon joining any pool, you work with other miners and try to solve that pool's existing block. In today's competitive mining environment, solving a block by yourself would require a very powerful and expensive hardware. When you are part of a pool the hashing power of all of the members will be used to solve blocks; the rewards will be split within all the members according to the amount of hash power each one contributed, making it a much more predictable and practical way of mining if you don't happen to have invested a fortune in mining hardware.

THE SYSTEM

Now, let's move on to understanding how the Bitcoin system works.

To get started, you need to install a digital/ Bitcoin wallet either on your mobile phone or computer. The wallet is an open-source program/ software that will begin generating your Bitcoin address. Once your first address has been created, you can make several more addresses later on or whenever you need a new one. You can tell your friends or clients your address so they can pay you.

To download a wallet simply visit bitcoin.org

There are basically four different types of wallets:

1. Software wallets - which are installed on your computer via a simple app.

2. Mobile wallets - which is an app for your mobile device.

3. Online or Cloud wallets – which are wallets stored on a server that you can access online.

4. Physical wallets – which are normally similar to USB drives that contain a software with your wallet and can have different security measures to grant access to your bitcoins.

Bitcoin makes use of public key cryptography for keeping the network safe and sound. This means that whenever a new address on Bitcoin is generated, an encrypted key pair containing private and public keys is also created. These pairs are long and unique strings comprising of numbers and letters.

Every address contains its separate Bitcoin balance. You can acquire numerous Bitcoins that will be held in the wallet. Bitcoins can be acquired in two basic forms:

1. By receiving them from other users.

2. By mining them using your computational power.

Every transaction that takes place contains three things: input, amount and output. Input is basically the record of the Bitcoin address that was employed for sending the Bitcoins. The amount refers to the quantity or number of bitcoins that are being sent and output refers to the address of the party receiving the Bitcoins.

All the Bitcoin transactions get stored permanently and publicly on the network. This means that transactions and balance of basically all the Bitcoin addresses are easily visible to all the users on the network. Experts advise that a Bitcoin owner should create a separate address for every transaction so its privacy can be ensured and the security can be further enhanced.

After you generate your Bitcoin address (addresses) and are done acquiring Bitcoins, you can make use of your Bitcoins for carrying out online transactions with any company or individual that recognizes Bitcoin as a mode of payment like you would with any other form of money.

The transaction normally takes a few seconds to take place, but its verification tends to take around ten minutes or even longer in certain cases. Confirmation or verification of a transaction takes a longer time as complex and intricate algorithms are involved in this process. This takes time to properly solve a block and add it to the Block chain.

All the Bitcoin transactions are contained in the Block chain, which is a transaction log made visible to the public, which means it is a shared log. This confirms that a party that is spending its Bitcoins is actually the owner. This also helps in preventing double spending and fraud.

Have a look at a Bitcoin transaction's example to better understand the system and how it works.

Assume that you are interested in carrying out an online transaction with a company called 'BitCoolDesigns'. You have to make a payment to them for a new logo design. You want to send 0.4 Bitcoins that you currently own in your Bitcoin digital wallet.

In this case, the record of the address you use for sending the five Bitcoins is the input. 0.4 Bitcoins is the amount and the output is the address of BitCoolDesigns to which you will be sending the five Bitcoins.

For this transaction to take place, first BitCoolDesigns will generate a fresh Bitcoin address. It will share with you the address so you can go on with the transaction.

Next, you command the Bitcoin client, which is your wallet, to move 0.4 Bitcoins to the address of BitCoolDesigns from your account/ wallet. This is known as 'transaction message'.

Your client wallet will sign that transaction request electronically using the address's private key from where you're transferring your Bitcoins. This is possible as your shared or freely available (public) key is actually known to anybody for practicing signature verification.

Your transaction then gets broadcasted to Bitcoin's network. It will be verified within a couple of minutes. The 0.4 Bitcoins are now transferred to BitPro's address from your account.

It is important to note that the basic first step demands action by your seller and the second one requires action from your end. The Bitcoin network and client software (wallet) executes the rest of the steps automatically.

At times, you need to wait for your transaction to become clear. This happens because a transaction needs to be verified and authenticated by miners and it takes them time to carry out mining at times. Certain merchants make you hang around until you can use their service or download their digital goods you have paid for. There are merchants who don't require you to wait for the transaction to get confirmed. They assume that you will not spend those Bitcoins anywhere else before that transaction becomes complete and trust you. This normally is true for transaction of low value or those where the fraud risk isn't huge.

Transaction Fees

Transaction fees do exist, but it is charged sometimes. It is calculated by considering different factors. Some wallets allow you to set a transaction fee manually. Part of a certain transaction that is not returned or picked by your recipient is considered as the fee. This amount is transferred to that particular miner who was working on your transaction block.

Are Receipts Issued?

Initially receipts weren't issued on Bitcoin. However, different changes are coming in the program. Payment processors such as BitPay offer advanced and improved features that aren't provided to you when you make a traditional Bitcoin transaction. These features include getting an order confirmation webpage and receipts.

CAN YOU SEND A SMALL PART OF BITCOIN?

You can divide a Bitcoin transaction to a very tiny amount. One Satoshi refers to one Bitcoin's one hundred millionth portion. Therefore, it is true that you can send a tiny part of a Bitcoin. In fact, you can send transactions as tiny as 0.0000001 of a Bitcoin.

MINING

Although this chapter will explains what mining really is about in a technical way, so you have a better understanding of a vital part of the Bitcoin system; it's important to notice that in a much broader way, mining is the foundation of Bitcoin's computing power.

Since Bitcoin is a decentralized currency that doesn't rely on a specific single system or person, it needs a network of nodes of computing power to serve it to complete all the millions of heavily encrypted and complex transaction calculations that happen every day at every second in order to keep the transaction system working.

MINERS provide this massive amount of computational power and they are simply other users, like you and me. That's why you, or anyone, can't access a centralized Bitcoin mainframe and shut it down. It's the same concept of the WWW, there are thousands of servers connected one to the other, so everyone provides a node to the network and the network is not dependant on any one single computer.

To become a miner you just need to download a piece of free software, connect to the Internet and run this software on your computer. Your computer then will become another node of Bitcoin's computational power, and will start to solve the mathematical problems needed to keep the Bitcoin's network running.

Every time your computer resolves one of these problems the system will give you a 25 Bitcoin reward. Of course this is easier said than done. Because a reward of 25 bitcoins has become so desirable a lot of people has specialized on running mining endeavours and building specific hardware to make mining profitable. So nowadays your home computer will not have the hardware requirements to make it a viable economical option.

It's important to say that mining is the only way new Bitcoins can be created.

However there are other roads you can take if you want to enter the mining world, and we will speak about them bellow.

TYPES OF MINING

There are basically two main kinds of mining: solo and pool. Solo mining refers to practicing mining on your own. You don't have help or assistance offered by anyone in this mining category. Though, it is a private and peaceful method and can help you earn a reward of a whopping 25 Bitcoins, it is indeed the harder of the two methods. It could take a solo miner numerous weeks, months or even years in earning actual Bitcoins as they are relying on their own hardware to accomplish the goal.

On the other hand, pool mining is a better and more convenient method of practicing mining. Using this method, you sign up with an account offered by any company that carries out groups of miners working together, and adding all their computational power to solve blocks. Such companies have their own hardware and software and group together mining efforts and skills of several miners' computers. Every miner gets a proportional amount of Bitcoins depending on how much computational power they provided to the pool. However, this is a better option for you as it increases your likelihood of earning more Bitcoins.

If you are interested in knowing more about mining pools a simple Google search will put you in the right direction. However, as with everything that has to do with money, I'd encourage you to investigate your mining pool before committing to them your expensive hardware power, so you are certain that they are honest pooling people.

If you want to invest in mining you can acquire your specific mining hardware and place it at your home or office and start your mining business. You can use hardware in pool or solo, depending on your hash power.

It's important to notice, if you want to enter the world of hardware mining, that due to the specifics of the Bitcoin market and the constant increase of difficulty on mining, the hardware that was seen as top of the line a year ago today is just a toy today that will eat electricity and produce little to no profit.

To make a profitable mining business you will need to calculate:

- The actual cost of the mining rig

- The Hash rate at which it will mine

- The cost of electricity

- Bitcoin difficulty

- Pool fees

Doing a simple Google search on "bitcoin mining calculator" will point you to many calculators that can help you determine how long you will take to recoup your investment, if you decided to invest in hardware.

Also take into consideration that the hardware is not available for buying immediately and should be ordered months in advance. This happens because at the moment the hardware is available should be immediately put to work since it will have the best chance of making it's cost back; hence it's put to work immediately. The developers and engineers then will go back to work to produce even better and more powerful hardware, which will take some time to accomplish.

I have done an effort to keep this list current, however this companies are constantly changing and closing. Again a simple Google search might do the trick. Some hardware brands you might find are:

- Alpha Technology

- Hash Fast

- Bitmain

- Buterfly Labs

You should do your own due diligence before committing on buying hardware, since it can be very expensive and companies that produce them are not always very reliable.

There are mainly three categories of hardware for miners: FPGAs, ASICs and GPUs.

FPGA refers to Field Programmable Gate Array, which is an incorporated circuit that needs to undergo configuration after it is built. It allows a hardware manufacturer in getting a large volume of chips that can be customized for mining before they are placed in the equipment. Due to their customizable features, they help you mine better than GPUs and CPUs.

ASIC refers to Application Specific Integrated Circuits. They are specifically created for one purpose: mining Bitcoins at an escalating speed without consuming a lot of power. Due to their excellent speed and low consumption of power, these chips are quite costly. Their speed ranges from 5 to 500 Gigahashes per second, which is a huge amount.

GPU and CPU mining refers to mining using your own computer. This is an extremely slow type of mining since your computer does not have enough power and speed to practice mining at an increasingly fast pace. Adding in graphic hardware in your computer can increase the hash rate using your CPU. This card consists of graphical processing units (GPUs) that are created for enormous mathematical lifting that helps them calculate complex polygons. The two major vendors of GPUs are NVidia and ATI. These high ends are pricey but help you practice CPU mining expediently and at a good pace too. This hardware is normally used to mine other types of currencies, like Litecoin since use a system that benefits from GPU mining.

If you are beginning and want to try your hand at mining, instead of buying hardware I'd much recommend to "rent" hash powers. There are companies that have huge facilities with top of the line hardware that is already set up for mining; that can be a much easier solution since you will rent the computational power and configure it to deposit your bitcoins directly into your wallets. This practice is known as "cloud mining". As stated before if you want to rent hash power please be advised to take a good look at who you are sending your money too.

How mining exactly works (only if you want to get a deeper understanding on this subject)

People send Bitcoins to one another using the Bitcoin network 24/7. Nobody can keep note of what they paid to whom unless somebody actually maintains records of all those transactions. Bitcoin's network comes to your rescue at this point and helps you keep proper track of all the transaction by collecting and arranging them in a list that is known as a block. Mining is basically the activity that is executed for confirming those transactions as well as writing them in a ledger.

Mining is an activity carried out to ascertain the network's security. The main concept is that miners of Bitcoin group a number of the Bitcoin transactions that took place in a certain time in a block and then execute cryptographic operations, known as hashing, numerous times till someone discovers a rare and unique hash value. Hashing does not achieve anything productive itself, but it ascertains that nobody can take over Bitcoin's system, as identifying successful blocks is an extremely difficult task.

The ledger, also known as 'general ledger' basically contains a list of different blocks that is known as 'Block-chain.' It is employed to discover any transaction that has been carried out between any of the addresses on Bitcoin at any time on Bitcoin's network. When a fresh block containing transactions gets generated, it is appended to a block-chain and creates an extensive and long list of every transaction that has ever taken place on Bitcoin's network. An updated and efficient copy of that block is provided to all those who are participating to keep them up-to-date with the happenings. It is imperative that a certain block chain is not interfered with and stays intact. This is the point where the hardworking miners come in helpful.

Whenever a block containing transactions gets generated, the miners make it go through a certain process. They extract the information contained in that block, apply a complex mathematically formula on it and encrypt it. The result is a random and shorter string comprising of numerous numbers and letters and is referred to as 'hash.' The hash is then stored in the block and lies at the block-chain's end.

Hashes contain interesting properties. A hash can be easily produced using a compilation of data such as Bitcoin block. However, it is actually impossible to tell what that data really was by staring at that hash. It is convenient to generate hash using a colossal data quantity, but every hash is completely unique. By changing a single character stored in one Bitcoin block, you alter the entire hash completely.

Miners use transactions contained in a particular block along with other data for creating a hash. For instance, hash of that last block that has been saved in a block-chain is needed for generating a new hash. As every block requires the previous block's hash, a digital form of wax seal is created. This confirms that, that particular block and each block created after that one is legitimate and if you tamper it, everyone will find it out.

If someone tries making a counterfeit transaction by altering any block that has been saved in a block-chain already, the hash of that block would change. If anyone examined that block's genuineness by running hashing function, they would find out that, that hash was dissimilar to the hash that had originally been stored in that block-chain. Instantly, a fake block would be spotted.

As every block's hash is used for producing the next block's hash, when someone tampers with a block, they infect the hash of the subsequent block as well. This continues down the entire chain and disrupts everything. However, courtesy of the miners, blocks gets properly sealed and the system does not become corrupted or infected.

All the miners are competing with one another for sealing blocks. They do this by making use of software that has been specifically created for mining blocks. Each time a miner created a successful hash, they are given 25 Bitcoins as reward. The block-chain gets updated and all those using the network find out about it as well. The reward is basically an incentive to motivate the miners to work harder so they can continue securing the network and enable the transactions to work properly.

An encrypted hash function utilizes one block consisting of the input data for creating unpredictable and smaller strings of output. The creation of hash function ensures that there is not any short cut for getting the preferred and desired output. You need to continue hashing blocks until you get one that actually works. Bitcoin makes use of the SHA-256 hash function. For increasing the network's security, Bitcoin uses this function twice and this process is referred to as 'double SHA-256.'

A strong and successful hash in Bitcoin is one starting with sufficient zeros. Just the way it is rare and hard to locate a license plate number or telephone number ending in several zeros, it is quite rare to come across and discover a hash that starts with numerous zeros. Currently, a good hash needs to begin with at least 17 zeros. That means that one of 1.4×10^{20} hashes has a chance of being successful. Therefore, discovering one successful hash is tougher than identifying one certain sand grain from all the sand grains in the world.

Another problem is that the moment a certain data piece is added, the hash comes out to be entirely different so the miners' job is an extremely tough one. Miners must not meddle with any part of the transaction information in a certain block. However, they need to alter that data which they are using so they can generate a dissimilar hash. This is then amalgamated with the data of the transaction for creating a hash.

In case the hash fails to fit the desired format, the miners change the nonce and the entire thing needs to be hashed once more. It can take myriads of attempts in finding a workable nonce. Plus, every miner on the network is working towards achieving this goal simultaneously. This is a demanding job indeed, but it is what enables the miners in earning their Bitcoins.

BUYING AND SELLING

There are different ways of purchasing and selling Bitcoins. Look at the variety of exchanges you can opt for when buying or selling Bitcoins.

There are two main methods of selling and procuring Bitcoins: selling/ buying in person or buying/ selling online. Each of the two options has its own share of pros and cons.

ONLINE METHOD

Selling and purchasing Bitcoins online is a commonly practiced method of trading Bitcoins. There are three common ways of getting your bitcoins online:

1. DIRECT TRADE

Websites that provide you platforms for online trading include Bittylicious and BitBargain in the U.K and LocalBitcoins and Coinbase in the U.S. You need to get registered as a Bitcoin seller for trading on these sites. You would need to verify your identity for registering yourself. Most of the markets practicing Bitcoin trading don't demand an extensive verification from the buyers, but aren't that lenient with the sellers. They consider your joining date on the website, require you to give scans of any two (utility) bills that display your complete address and name along with your photo ID (your driving license or passport.) if you aren't comfortable giving your personal documents, then you would experience a lot of difficulty in selling Bitcoins online.

After your registration is complete, you can begin posting offers online that would signal that you plan to sell Bitcoins. The site will send you notifications alerting you when any buyer is interested in trading with you. After that, you and the buyer will be solely responsible for the transaction, but you will be using the site as a platform for completing the trade.

Bitcoins users in the U.S. who have their individual bank accounts should consider trading on Circle or Coinbase as these websites are user-friendly and help you trade easily.

3. EXCHANGE TRADES

Another way you can sell and buy Bitcoins is by registering with an exchange online. You would need to confirm your identity. However, you won't be required to work a lot for organizing a sale. These exchanges work as intermediaries that hold the funds of people trading on them. You need to put up a 'sell or buy order', state the amount and the currency type you want to sell or buy as well as the per unit price of that currency you are planning on trading. That currency will be credited soon to the account in your name.

While using any exchange, you would be required to pay some fee for using that exchange's services. BTC-e has a flat fee of 0.2 percent. In addition to that, there is a limit on the volume of money that you can store on a certain exchange. This is why experts advise that you don't store all your money (Bitcoins) on an exchange. It is best to store additional funds on any of your personal devices instead of keeping it on any exchange that has a risk of getting hacked, goes bankrupt or losing it's banking connections.

PEER-TO-PEER TRADING

The third method of exercising online trading of Bitcoins is by making use of 'peer-to-peer trading places and venues.' These are basically websites that bring together groups of traders with similar and opposite needs. One group comprises of those individuals who are interested in using Bitcoins for buying goods from websites that don't accept any digital currency directly. The second group consists of people who want to purchase Bitcoins using a debit or credit card. Trading marketplaces give these people a platform where they can sell Bitcoins offer discounted goods to each other, respectively.

Such marketplaces are basically working as intermediaries providing users with a proper platform to execute the trade, escrow for carrying out the transactions and Bitcoin wallets.

Look at an example to understand how this method works. Amy posts her Amazon wish list on a peer-to-peer trading marketplace and states that she would prefer discounts up to 25 percent. Ben owns a debit/ credit card and is interested in purchasing Bitcoins that match the exact value of Amy's purchases. He agrees to that trade via the marketplace and purchases the respective goods Amy is interested in and requests Amazon that those goods be delivered on the address given by Amy. As soon as the order is delivered, Amy notifies that marketplace and Ben's Bitcoins get released from the escrow. They are then transferred to Ben's wallet minus the agreed discount by Amy as well as a fee charged by the marketplace.

There are certain concerns pertinent to withdrawing funds using online methods. You can move your money around using the international method of wire transfers. The majority of the Bitcoin markets working online support this procedure.

You can also make use of the SEPA system, which stands for Single European Payments Area. It was created to execute transfers internationally between the member states and countries of the EU (European Union). Exchanges such as BTC-e and Kraken recognize this method. However, transfers tend to take quite a long time that can extend up to four to five days. They can also incur huge charges that make the trading extremely costly. HSBC charges around £4 on every SEPA payment that is executed using online banking. Barclays charges around £15 on every SEPA payment.

Some exchanges like Coinbase will connect directly to your US bank account, making it very easy to trade fiat money, like USD to BTC and back.

Direct Selling

Direct selling or selling Bitcoins in person to a buyer is another way you can sell and buy Bitcoins. This is quite an easy method of passing on the digital currency you own. You need to scan the QR code using the other person's mobile phone for accepting the cash-in-hand. If there are family members, friends or colleagues who are interested in purchasing Bitcoins then you can easily practice this method. Set the concerned buyers with any Bitcoin wallet, transfer Bitcoins to their account and collect the cash amount.

However, you need to take care of a few things when practicing direct Bitcoin trading.

- Settle on a Suitable Rate: You need to decide a certain rate that would work well for you. Most of the sellers take a price using well-known Bitcoin exchanges such as Bitcoin Price Index or CoinDesk. Some sellers may apply a certain percentage on these rates for covering costs or as anonymity premium. You can take the assistance of mobile application for calculating the prices. Popular and workable apps include BTCreport and Zeroblock. It is important that you are aware of the local fluctuations occurring in the price. Price tends to vary from one country to another, mainly due to problems in acquiring

Bitcoins using the national currency of that country. Various Bitcoin meet-ups take place across the globe where people interested in trading cyrptocurrencies and Bitcoins meet with concerned people and execute different trades.

- Safety Issues: Don't forget that Bitcoin is real money and once the transaction took place there's no way of reverting it, so be careful like you would if moving big sums of cash.

LOCALBITCOINS

LocalBitcoins is a website where you can broadcast your identity as a seller of Bitcoin to a large audience. This is another method to exercise Bitcoin trading. The website allows all the users to rate one another so that people can assess the honestly, reliability and trustworthiness of different trade partners to choose a dependable one. Once you are successful in establishing a reliable reputation on the site, you can sell Bitcoins with a certain premium. It is a convenient mode of practicing Bitcoin trading as you aren't demanded to prove your identity like you had to do on the other websites discussed above. If you plan on setting a direct meeting with a buyer you identified on LocalBitcoins, you need to observe safety precautionary measures so that you aren't scammed. LocalBitcoins does support and recognize escrow transactions, but these are limited to be used for the online transactions and not the direct dealings. Hence, you must not comply with any requests from a person who asks you for a direct escrow transaction.

ALTERNATIVE CURRENCIES TO BITCOIN

Several other digital currencies are being used and traded in the market. After watching the enormous success of Bitcoin, many programmers decided to make their own Alternative Currencies, so it seems like everyday there is a new one. However here are nine different alternatives to Bitcoin that are now slowly coming in the limelight.

- Litecoin: This is a digital currency based on cryptography that makes it similar to Bitcoin. Its value has experienced quite a dramatic rise recently. An open source peer-to-peer digital currency is often termed as Bitcoin's spin-off. Its operations use Bitcoin's protocol as the foundation, but Litecoin can be easily mined using the standard computers as it algorithm was created by Dr. Colin Percival to be used on different open source computers and operating systems.

- Peercoin: It is another popular variant of Bitcoin. It promises its users with enhanced mining efficiency, better security and improved group mining. It is the fourth biggest alternative digital currency of Bitcoin and its market is growing with each passing day.

- Namecoin: A cryptocurrency can work as a dispersed DNS. As Namecoin acts as the currency's own DNS, it can operate outside of the internet and Icann (Internet Corporation for Assigned Names and Numbers) easily. The domain names and currency values are saved in the record of the block-chain that limits Namecoin's total number to 21m. Each coin can be divided to around eight decimal points.

- Feathercoin: Feathercoin is based on Litecoin and the mining difficulty of this currency is frequently adjusted. It makes regular updates to the software for adding new enhancements and features to it such as protections against forking and abuse in group mining that is one of the most serious concerns in group mining.

- Primecoin: It is a cryptocurrency like the famous Bitcoin, but it employs an entirely separate mathematical procedure for mining that makes it different than Bitcoin. It does not rely on the Hashcash algorithm that is used by Bitcoin. Instead, it uses the long Cunningham strings for building value of the currency. Cunningham chains are sequences comprising of different prime numbers and have been named after AJC Cunningham, a renowned mathematician. The difficult level of Primecoin's mining is higher than that of Bitcoin mining.

- Novacoin: Novacoin is a peer-to-peer digital currency that integrates protections schemes in the currency's core to deter abuse occurring in the mining groups. Its technical cap of around 2bn coins that is a larger value than the technical cap of the majority of the other currencies that tops out in millions and not billions.

- Infinitecoin: It is yet another spin-off of Litecoin, but differs from its ancestor in two ways. First, its mining difficulty rate is adjusted quite frequently and more coins can be easily created in Infinitecoin. Currently, one can generate around 1142.86 times more coins as those created in Litecoin.

- Megacoin: It was created during the end of 2013 and is in its growing phase currently. It comprises of 42m coins at the moment and each coin is valued at $0.50.

- Quark coin: It is another digital currency that is in the infancy stage right now. It takes security issues very seriously and has employed nine different encryption grounds by making use of six dissimilar algorithms to enhance the network's protection and security.

In addition to these nine popular substitutes of Bitcoin, there are myriads of other digital currencies that are being traded in the market. These include AlphaCoin, AnonCoin, BBQCoin, AmericanCoin, AndroidsTokens, BitGem, BitCar, AsicCoin, BottleCaps, CopperLark, CHNCoin, CryptogenicBullion, CryptoBuck, CasinoCoin, CopperBars, ColossusCoins, CryptogenicBullion, CopperLark, CraftCoin, ByteCoin and CryptoBuck.

The reason why there is a massive number altcoins, growing every day, is because after the big success of bitcoin, a lot of people wants to emulate it by creating their won altcurrency an hence being there from the beginning. However a big number of this coins will eventually fail.

WALLETS

As you probably know by now, your wallet will be the place where you will store your bitcoins. Its main purpose will be to store the private keys of your Bitcoin addresses as well as taking record of all the transactions you will conduct. But in a more practical sense, you will use it to send, receive and store your bitcoins.

You don't need to have only one wallet, you could see it more like a bank account and have one for spending or trading and one for saving or even one for traveling, one for home and one for long term savings, depending on your personal situation.

However there are different kind of wallets and they have their uses and purposes, so it's very important that you know how each one of these operate so you can decide what's better for your particular situation.

Remember that the bitcoins that you might have will be stored in a particular wallet, and if for any reason you loose it (let's say you have it in your hard drive on your laptop), and for example your laptop falls from a cliff and the hard drive gets damage and becomes unrecoverable, your Bitcoins will be lost FOREVER, there will be no way of getting them back. So I believe it's of high importance to decide where and how you will store your hard earned bitcoins and also strategies to back up them.

A simple way to get started with Wallets and download some of them is to visit bitcoin.org and head to the "Wallets" section.

BITCOIN DESKTOP WALLETS

(Armory, Hive (OS X), MultiBit (Windows, OS X and Linux), DarkWallet). These are some of the most popular Desktop wallets. As their name implies, these are wallets that are basically a piece of software that you download to your computer and keep it there.

With this software you can create bitcoin addresses to send and receive bitcoins and also store them.

They have the great advantage of being in your own computer, and thus they are very secure, the limitation is that if something happens to your hard drive, your computer gets lost, etc. You will lose them forever.

Also if you are, for example traveling, and you need bitcoin that is stored at your computer back home it will be impossible to retrieve them at the moment you need them.

However because of it's safety and easy of use, the Desktop Wallet option is one of the most popular among bitcoin users.

BITCOIN MOBILE WALLETS

Here you can find the likes of Mycelium, Blockchain and Xapo. These wallets are pieces of software to be installed on your smartphone. As you might have already guessed, they are great to move around with bitcoin and even use the benefit of (NFC) Near Field Communication, which allows you to pay or get paid simply by tapping on the phone without the need of entering any information. However the obvious disadvantage of mobile wallets lies in its portability. If the smart phone is lost the bitcoin will be lost too.

BITCOIN ONLINE WALLETS

Here you can find Coinbase, Blockchain and Xapo. These wallets are held on the Internet by some third party. They have the great advantage of being always available and not being dependant of any single device in your control. You can access them from anywhere you can find an Internet connection and if your wallet provider is a reputable one they can be very secure.

Other benefit is that you can use them to duplicate (or backup) your addresses from mobile or desktop wallets.

However the great disadvantage of these wallets is that you involve a third party: the wallet provider. Someone else will be in control of your funds and somehow you will be disabling the whole purpose of bitcoin, bringing yourself back to centralization

PHYSICAL WALLETS OR PAPER WALLETS

As the name implies, these wallets are physical representation of your Bitcoin addresses, they are a printed piece of paper with two QR codes, the first containing your Bitcoin address and the second one to encrypt your private key.

They have the great advantage of not depending on any online service or computer, thus they are immune to hacking. However they become a target for physical theft. In case a robber know this piece of paper is of any value, they could take it from you and relieve you from your bitcoins. They are not useful for receiving or sending bitcoin and must be seen more of a long-term storage solution for your bitcoin.

HARDWARE WALLETS

These wallets are pieces of software stored on a physical device (like a USB pen drive) with some added security features; like password protections and some encryption. You can store your bitcoins in one of these devices with a little more safety than a normal USB pen drive. Some of them will even allow you to send and receive bitcoins securely by connecting them to an online device.

You must remember that no matter what wallet type you decide to use, they are all attached to your private key (password), you will need to enter this password to access your bitcoin, and currently there is no password recovery in Bitcoin, so if your password is lost your bitcoin will be lost too. It's also very important to choose strong passwords to encrypt your wallet and reduce the possibility of hacking.

It's a good practice to backup your wallets and make a printable version to keep with your valuable things. A desktop wallet can also be stored in a physical drive like a USB pen drive and be kept away from your Internet connected personal computer.

TRADING BITCOIN

Ok, so you heard somewhere that trading Bitcoin with leverage would be a good idea. Let me tell you, it won't. You could make boatloads of money exchanging cryptocurrencies back and forth (or lose it), and I will give you in this chapter a technique I use to make some regular gains in bitcoins or litecoins or any of the thousands of cryptocoins that you can find in this crazy realm at some point, although I don't do it anymore nor endorse it, so if you are going to try it do it at your own risk.

However I wouldn't advice anyone to risk his or her money on trading, especially money you can't afford to lose. So if you try these techniques don't do it because I am telling you, I only print this information for academic and informative reasons and not to encourage anyone to trade currency.

Please contact a professional advisor before trading your hard earned money, I don't accept any responsibility for the use you give to the information that I am about to share; what you do with this information and / or if you lose any money trading I will take no liability what so ever.

Ok, so if after all the discouragement you still want to read about Bitcoin Trading... here we go:

The idea on trading anything, and Bitcoin in particular, is to buy cheap and sell expensive, or to buy low and sell high.

So what are we trading anyway? we will be trading the exchange difference between two altcurrencies, let's say we buy Litecoins with our Bitcoins; after a few hours, if our trading was right, the Litecoin might have gained a few points, so we sell it back to buy Bitcoin and make money on the difference. Then we go and look for the next opportunity, and we keep on doing this until we are fed up with millions of altcoins.

So how exactly can you do this?

First go to your Coinbase account and buy a few bitcoins or small fractions of bitcoins, start small to practice, you can increase your exposure later once you are profitable and you understand the process.

Then you want to sign up for exchanges, you can use cryptsy.com and exmo.com to start with, however you will need to have accounts in many more exchanges, as you'll see in a minute. In these exchanges you will be able to buy and sell a wide number of altcoins and you will have an address to receive your bitcoin from your Coinbase account or your wallet so you can start trading.

Ok, next you can find a list of the altcoins market's share and in which exchanges to find them here:

www.coinmarketcap.com.

There you will find a table with the different altcoins and also the amount of VOLUME they are trading. You should sort them out by the volume as the sorting criteria, because you should only trade currencies that have at least $40,000 of volume for the day or more. On any given day there could be between 12 and 20 within this range.

We do this because we want to buy and sell easily and not get stuck with some thinly traded coin that no one will take from us when we want to sell it. You really want to be where the traders are and take advantage of the Volume of transactions in a specific coin.

So we will be looking for volume spikes, for that we will use the column named % Change (24h). In this column we can see the hottest coins and the ones we're interested in buying.

For example right now as I am writing this lines I can see Nautiluscoin going up like crazy, 90.72% in the last 24 hours!

| 76 | ○ NautilusCoin | $ 378,264 $ 0.071074 | 5,322,099 NAUT | $ 41,872 | 90.72 % | |

So I go and check in which exchange I can find this atlcoin:

I click on the coin can see they have it on Bittrex, Criptsy and Poloniex.

○ **NautilusCoin** (NAUT)   **$ 0.070424** (88.78 %)
0.00026196 BTC (86.45 %)

◊ Website	
Q Explorer	
◄ Discussion	

Market Cap	Volume (24h)	Available Supply
$ 374,804	$ 41,961	5,322,099 NAUT
1,394 BTC	156 BTC	

.ıl Charts   ⇄ Markets   ◉ Social

NautilusCoin Markets

Main Markets ▾   USD ▾

#	Source	Pair	Volume (24h)	Price	Volume (%)	Updated
1	Bittrex	NAUT/BTC	$ 33,406	$ 0.069891	79.61 %	Recently
2	Cryptsy	NAUT/BTC	$ 6,979	$ 0.071999	16.63 %	Recently
3	Poloniex	NAUT/BTC	$ 1,576	$ 0.074741	3.76 %	Recently

But as you can see the volume, and the price is much better on Bittrex, so I rush to Bittrex and open an account (it should be ready in a few minutes) and deposit the bitcoins I want to use to trade.

So by now we know:

1. How to identify possible coins to trade - go to coinmarketcap.com and sort them by volume

2. Which ones can be candidates – the ones that have over $40,000 of 24h volume

3. Pinpoint the one that can give us profits – The one that is having a crazy positive spike in the last 24h, anything over 40% or 50% can do the trick

4. Find the altcoin's market – click at the coin on the table and you can find in which markets it's trading and at what price, go for the highest volume and the best price.

5. Move our trading coins to the exchange and get ready to trade

Ok, we will stop here for a second to understand a bit better why we chose coins with price and volume spikes.

In this trading strategy we will normally tend to follow the trend, or what other traders are doing; so if people rushes to buy a specific coin we will rush to buy it too, we don't care for the reasons of this sudden interest. We only know that for now there is a mania for such coin that went nuts in a short amount of time and we want to capitalize on that mania.

It's important to understand that we're not buying for the long term. This sudden interest could last only a few hours or a few days, that's fine for us, we will stay in the trade only for a few minutes or hours and then get out with a profit.

We don't want to be the first one to jump into the pool or the last one. We just detect where the flow is going and take advantage of it for a little while and then go out. On a single trade you could make anywhere from 5 to 10% or more of your capital in a few hours, so the potential is really huge.

Ok so now let's trade those coins! let's say we have 1 bitcoin to trade. In Bittrex the exchange rate is $ 0.069891 so we can buy a

14.3079 Nautiluscoins with our 1 Bitcoin.

However please don't follow into the trap of thinking that you'll have to buy your shiny new Nautiluscoin for the "last price" found on the price rates.

You will see there's a list with all the people bidding and offering different amounts of coin. You must try to low-ball the offer as much as possible. In all the exchanges you will find a table like this with the buy orders and sell orders, in this table you will find what is people paying to buy and sell their coins.

As you can see, trading will require a lot of time and commitment from your part, try not to over do it and it's better if you start with low expectations and risking little money until you feel confident about what you're doing.

🏷 Sell Orders

Price (BTC)	NAUT	Total (BTC)
0.00035998	1192.05909188	0.42911743
0.00035999	0.80114411	0.00028840
0.00036000	1.71684073	0.00061806
0.00036874	0.12400000	0.00004572
0.00037000	294.72626254	0.10904872
0.00038000	0.12400000	0.00004712
0.00038980	300.12400000	0.11698834
0.00038992	500.12400000	0.19500835
0.00040000	15000.84129661	6.00033652
0.00041020	104.94788555	0.04304962

🏷 Buy Orders

Price (BTC)	NAUT	Total (BTC)
0.00033025	154.16614260	0.05091337
0.00033011	2.76686133	0.00091337
0.00033010	130.00000000	0.04291300
0.00033000	650.00000000	0.21450000
0.00030922	19.40366082	0.00600000
0.00030920	202.35417694	0.06256791
0.00030913	2935.30826359	0.90739184
0.00030751	11.66763427	0.00358791
0.00030161	9987.65333701	3.01237612
0.00027000	1200.00000000	0.32400000

So once you have bought your Altcoins you only have to sit and wait to see if the market keeps rising, normally it will and after one hour or maybe two or even three you will have a profit. However I'd never recommend going away from your screen leaving your trade open, if you go to sleep or need to do something just buy back your Bitcoin and stay safe.

If things go wrong and you start to lose money, pick a number you are willing to lose every time, let's say 10% as an example, and if price just go against you and hit that price point simply sell and buy back your Bitcoins, don't worry, you'll have plenty of opportunities to recover.

CONCLUSION

By now, you must have understood what Bitcoin is, how it operates, what terminologies you need to be aware of for understanding this digital currency, how you can buy and sell Bitcoins, how you can invest in this cryptocurrency and what setbacks are involved in it.

Let's discuss how Bitcoin can benefit you before concluding the book.

- Low Risk of Inflation: All the paper currencies in the world are experiencing the inflation issue. With time, every currency tends to lose its purchasing power as the governments continue to print more money. However, this issue does not arise with Bitcoin. This is because only a finite amount of Bitcoins can be generated. Currently, this value is 21 million. Less Bitcoins are being released as time passes. By the time 2050 arrives, only 10 billion Bitcoins will be produced that means that there'll be one Bitcoin per 500 people.

- Low Risk of Collapse: Regular currencies are entirely dependent on the different governments for their success and failure. Failure of a certain government can result in a particular currency's collapse and can wipe it out of the market. This is where Bitcoin differs from such currencies. It is a virtual currency used all across the globe and is not dependent on any government in particular.

- Cheap, Simple and Safe: Different payment systems used online allows the buyers to ask for their money after a payment has been made. This does not happen with Bitcoin. Once you receive an amount of money, you won't be asked to return it. This provides sellers with increased safety of enjoying the money they earned as their buyers cannot claim it once they have paid the amount. Due to peer-to-peer functioning of the platform, buyers are able to enjoy a cheaper and simpler mode of paying money.

- Anonymity: You have complete liberty of maintaining your anonymity while carrying out a transaction. No company or buyer can track the exact source of your funds, so you don't need to be concerned about this issue when using Bitcoins.

- Convenience of Carrying: Carrying Bitcoins worth billions of dollars is not a problem at all. Use a memory stick to carry as many Bitcoins as you want at one time without worrying about getting robbed.

- No Interruptions by a Third Party: No third parties such as financial intermediaries, governments or banks bother you when you use Bitcoins. Being a peer-to-peer system, Bitcoin enables you to enjoy using the currency easily.

- No Tax Added to Your Purchases: As the transaction cannot be intercepted or tracked by any third party, no sales tax is appended to any of the purchases you make using Bitcoin. This helps you save all that money that was otherwise going to be cut as tax if you weren't using digital currency.

- Mobile Payments: You do not need to make Bitcoin payments by going to any financial institution or a bank. As wallets can be downloaded on your phone, you can easily make Bitcoin payments using your mobile phone.

- Small Transaction Fee: As no intermediary is involved in Bitcoin transactions, the transaction fee is relatively smaller as compared to that of wire transfers. This is a great benefit for the travelers.

To enjoy these advantages offered by Bitcoin, you need to step into the world of Bitcoin and become a part of this innovative and dynamic network. By now you are fully knowledgable of what technicalities are involved while using Bitcoin and how you can get yourself registered with it. Now, you need to take a bold step forward and get a Bitcoin wallet. Downloading it on your mobile phone or computer is an extremely easy and convenient procedure. You should use a wallet type that you find most convenient to operate. Next, you need to look for goods or services that can be bought with Bitcoins and begin trading.

You have been informed of what drawbacks can affect you and how you can benefit from Bitcoin. Therefore, you need to consider that knowledge when using Bitcoins. The best thing about using Bitcoins is that you need not have any skill or knowledge for utilizing this digital currency. It is just like using any kind of paper money.

However, if you are planning on venturing into Bitcoin mining, then you need to consider several important things. Bitcoin mining is a complex procedure like it has been described before in the book. One needs to have a good amount of knowledge for entering a field as intricate and tough as Bitcoin mining. If you do feel at ease with this procedure then you need to work on what type of mining will suit you best. The three major types of mining have been elaborately discussed in the previous chapters so you need to pick one keeping that knowledge in mind.

Thank You!

I want to personally thank you for reading all the way to the end of my book. Please visit my website at:

http://alurapublishing.com/markjanniro ←You will find my free reports there

If you liked my book you will make a great service to other future customers by leaving your opinion on the Amazon site.

www.ingramcontent.com/pod-product-compliance
Lightning Source LLC
Chambersburg PA
CBHW051333170526
45166CB00002B/799

* 9 7 8 1 5 1 9 2 8 4 5 2 5 *